I0814875

XTREME HORROR LAB

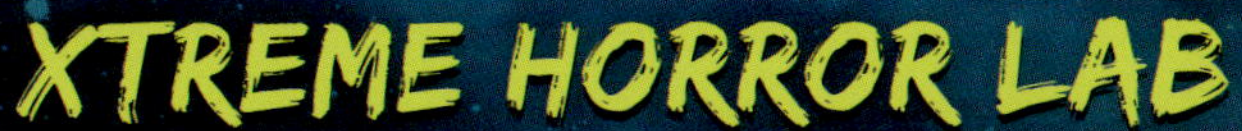

THE SCIENCE OF WEREWOLVES

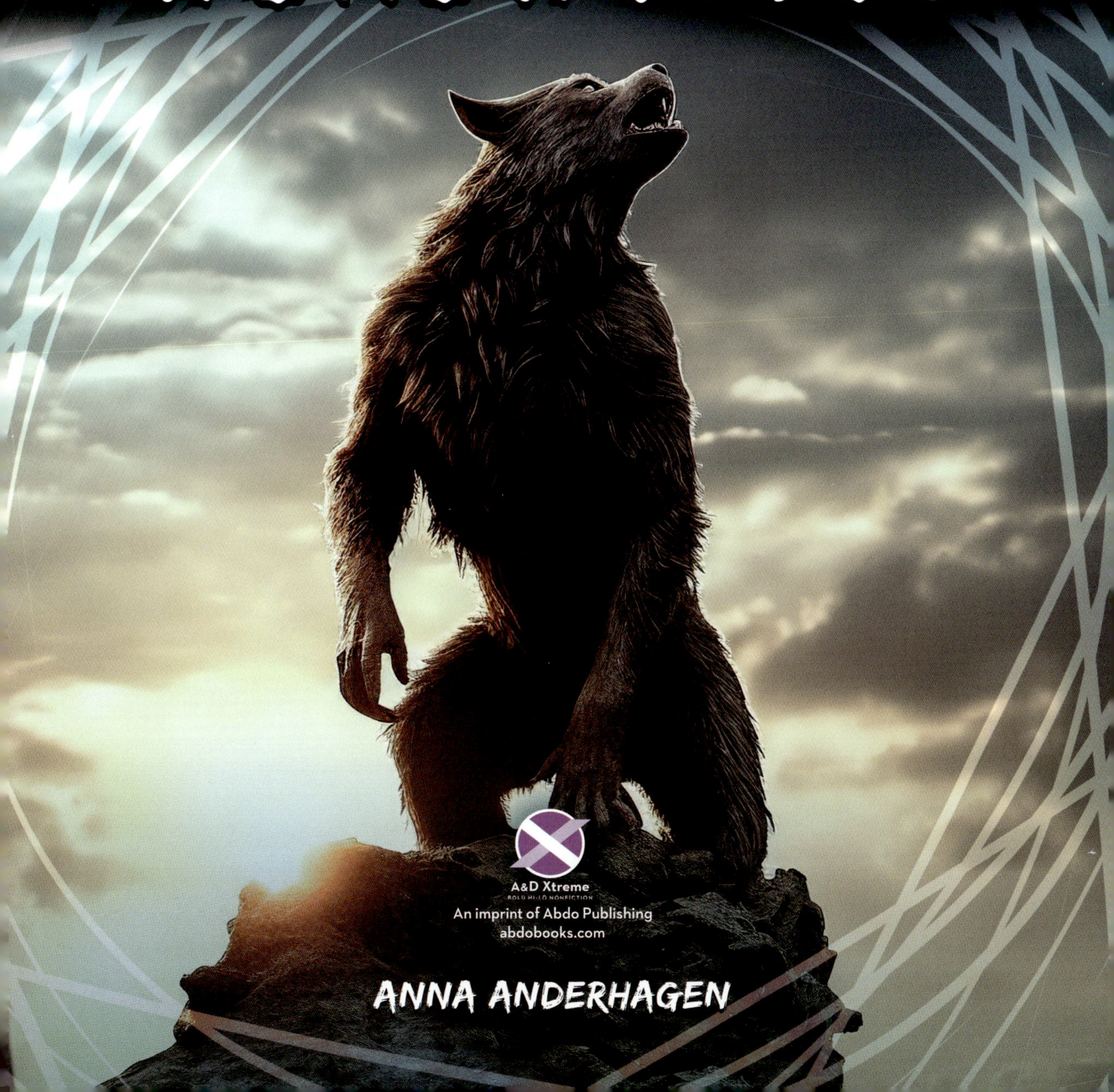

A&D Xtreme
BOLD HI-LO NONFICTION
An imprint of Abdo Publishing
abdobooks.com

ANNA ANDERHAGEN

TAKE IT TO THE XTREME!

GET READY FOR AN EXTREME ADVENTURE! THE PAGES OF THIS BOOK WILL TAKE YOU INTO THE SPOOKY WORLD OF UNEXPLAINED PHENOMENA. WHEN YOU HAVE FINISHED READING THIS BOOK, TAKE THE XTREME CHALLENGE ON PAGE 43 ABOUT WHAT YOU'VE LEARNED!

ABDOBOOKS.COM
Published by Abdo Publishing, a division of ABDO, PO Box 398166, Minneapolis, Minnesota 55439.

Printed in the United States of America, North Mankato, MN.
052024
092024

Design: Kelly Doudna, Mighty Media, Inc.
Production: Mighty Media, Inc.
Editor: Jessica Rusick
Cover Photograph: Jacques Evangelista/Adobe Stock
Interior Photographs: Alexander Tekuchev /Adobe Stock, p. 45 andreiuc88/Shutterstock Images, pp. 26–27; Ann Tyurina/Shutterstock Images, pp. 22–23; Chronicle/Alamy Photo, pp. 14–15; DanieleGay/Shutterstock Images, pp. 4–5; FANFAN/Adobe Stock, pp. 6–7; Harry Wedzinga/Adobe Stock, p. 44; Hendrik Goltzius/Wikimedia Commons, pp. 12-13; herle_catharina/Shutterstock Images, pp. 36–37; hespasoft/Adobe Stock, pp. 24-25; Hoefnagel, Joris/Wikimedia Commons, pp. 34–35; Jacques Evangelista/Adobe Stock, p. 1; kochanowski/Shutterstock Images, pp. 18–19; Luke23/Shutterstock Images, pp. 16–17; Mimadeo/Shutterstock Images, pp. 10-11; Mont Sudbury/Wikimedia Commons, p. 24; mrjo/Shutterstock Images, p. 42; Photo 12/Alamy Photo, pp. 8-9; riocontribae/Shutterstock Images, pp. 38–39; Stephen Canino/Adobe Stock, pp. 40–41; The Metropolitan Museum of Art/Wikimedia Commons, p. 11; Wikimedia Commons, pp. 20-21, 28–29; William Kent/Wikimedia Commons, p. 37; XaMaps/Adobe Stock, pp. 32–33; ZUMA Press Inc/Alamy Photo, pp. 30–31
Design Elements: Dominik Hladik/Shutterstock Images (moon); nikiteev_konstantin/Shutterstock Images (curves); pixelparticle/Shutterstock Images (stars); pixssa/Shutterstock Images (stretchy circle)

LIBRARY OF CONGRESS CONTROL NUMBER: 2023949632

PUBLISHER'S CATALOGING-IN-PUBLICATION DATA
Names: Anderhagen, Anna, author.
Title: The science of werewolves / by Anna Anderhagen
Description: Minneapolis, Minnesota : Abdo Publishing, 2025 | Series: Xtreme horror lab | Includes online resources and index.
Identifiers: ISBN 9781098293246 (lib. bdg.) | ISBN 9798384912514 (ebook)
Subjects: LCSH: Werewolves--Juvenile literature. | Monsters--Juvenile literature. | Werewolves in motion pictures--Juvenile literature. | Science--Juvenile literature.
Classification: DDC 130--dc23

TABLE OF CONTENTS

CHAPTER 1

FULL MOON

You are walking in the woods late one night. Suddenly, you hear a howl nearby. The hairs on your arms stand up. In the full moon's light, you see what looks like a half-man, half-wolf beast! It has long claws and fangs. You've heard of werewolves in movies and stories. But you never thought they could be real!

Werewolf sightings are reported each year in the United States. One wolflike creature nicknamed the Beast of Bray Road has been spotted in Wisconsin since the 1930s.

CHAPTER 2

TERRIFYING TERMINOLOGY

A werewolf is a creature from myth and legend. Werewolves are people that turn into wolves. This most often happens during a full moon. They return to human form by day. Werewolves are fierce hunters that attack animals and people. They are said to have powerful senses of hearing, taste, and smell.

In many legends, werewolves are not able to control when they transform. But some stories say werewolves can transform whenever they want.

XTREME FACT

Legend says you can stop a werewolf by shooting it with a silver bullet or yelling its human name.

According to modern stories, transforming into a werewolf is painful. Fingertips grow into claws. Teeth grow into fangs. Hair grows on the hands, feet, and face. The ears grow pointed and move back on the head.

In the 1981 film *An American Werewolf in London*, the main character undergoes a painful transformation into a werewolf.

Werewolves are **shape-shifters**. A shape-shifter is someone that can change into another being, usually an animal. People have told stories about shape-shifters since 13000 BCE. Many stories say that shape-shifters change into fierce animals at night. They turn back into humans at dawn. The most popular stories are about people who turned into wolves.

Werewolves have been depicted in many ways over the years. Often, they are entirely wolflike. But they have also been portrayed as looking human.

CHAPTER 3

WEREWOLVES OF THE PAST

Lycaon (*right*) is sometimes called the first werewolf.

Some of the early werewolf stories come from Greek **mythology**. Lycaon was king of ancient Greece around 380 BCE. He served Zeus a meal made of human flesh. Zeus was so angry that he turned Lycaon and his sons into wolves.

Another story comes from Norse **mythology**. It tells of a father and son who found wolf pelts. The pelts could turn people into wolves for 10 days. The father and son wore the pelts and became wolves. They killed many people in the forest.

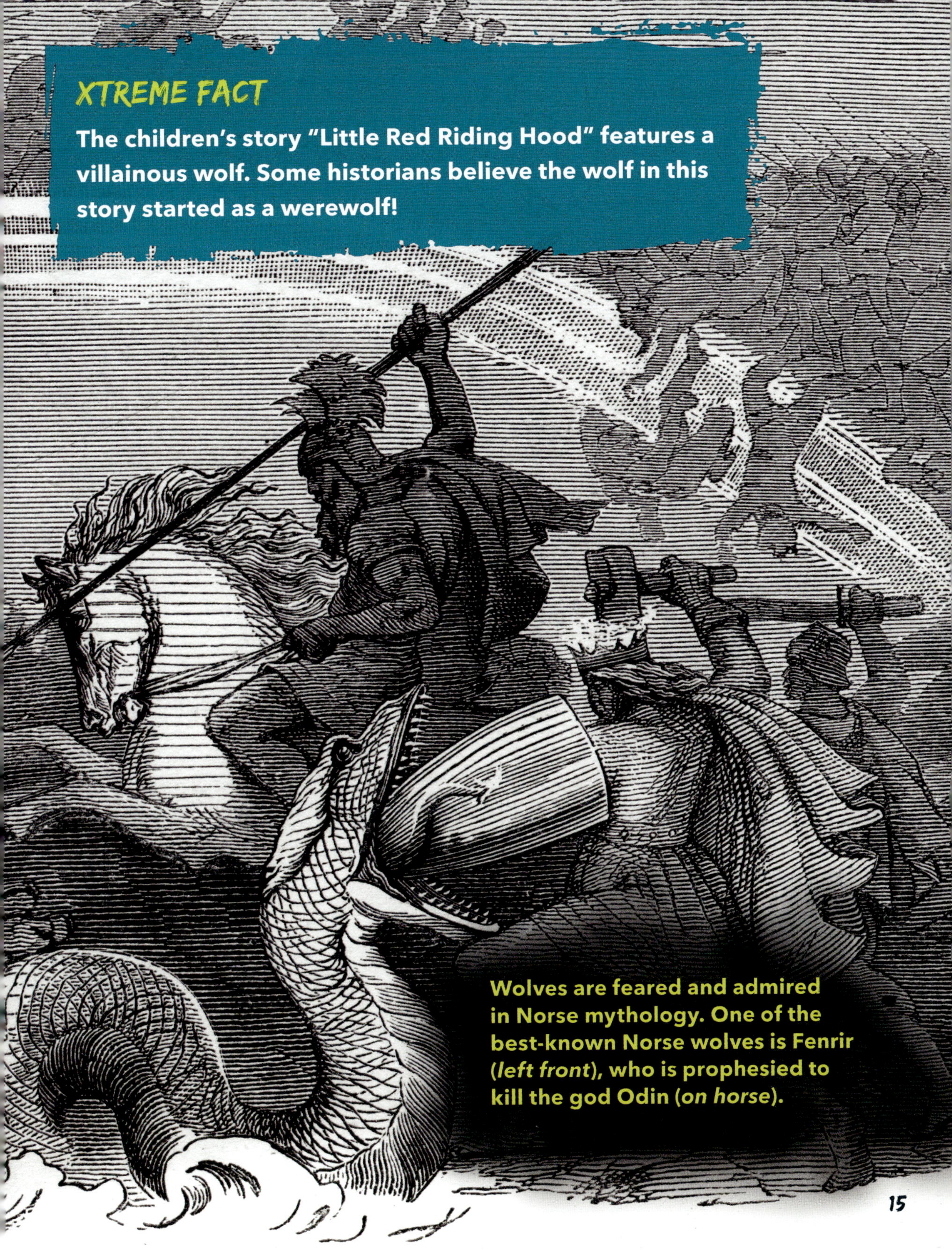

XTREME FACT

The children's story "Little Red Riding Hood" features a villainous wolf. Some historians believe the wolf in this story started as a werewolf!

Wolves are feared and admired in Norse mythology. One of the best-known Norse wolves is Fenrir (*left front*), who is prophesied to kill the god Odin (*on horse*).

Wolves are honored and respected in Navajo culture.

In Navajo myths, skinwalkers are people that can transform into animals. One of the most common animals is a wolf. Skinwalkers wear the skin of the animal they want to become. The Navajo told stories of skinwalkers bringing sickness and death to the Navajo people.

CHAPTER 4

BLAME THE BIG BAD WOLF

Werewolf stories likely grew from many humans' fear and dislike of wolves. Some historians say the hatred comes from wolves killing livestock. Wolves also have traits that scare humans. These traits include sharp teeth, sharp claws, and intelligence. Wolves are also feared for their loud howls.

Wolves have excellent senses of hearing and smell. They are skilled hunters that can track prey for hours.

Humans have connected wolves to evil and **witchcraft** in many cultures. In 1500s and 1600s Europe, someone who did an evil deed may have been accused

XTREME FACT

Torture is illegal under modern international law. It is also considered a bad way to get information. Innocent people admit to crimes they did not commit just to stop the torture.

of being a werewolf. There were thousands of werewolf trials during this time. Many people confessed to being werewolves, but usually only after they were **tortured**.

A werewolf is rumored to have terrorized Ansbach, Germany, in 1685. People in Ansbach believed the werewolf was their dead former mayor.

CHAPTER 5

WEREWOLVES IN EUROPE

In the 1580s, farmers in Bedburg, Germany, noticed that many cows were dying in their **pastures**. There was a rumor that a wolf was killing livestock. They described this wolf as having sharp teeth and huge paws.

Sheep are among the livestock most likely to be killed by wolves. Some farmers use sheepdogs to herd sheep and protect them from predators.

Stubbe said he made a pact with the devil to become a werewolf.

Then, people in Bedburg began to disappear and die. Some people thought a werewolf was responsible. In 1589, farmer Peter Stubbe was accused of being the werewolf. After he was **tortured**, Stubbe confessed.

Bedburg is a town near the western boundary of Germany. Germany shares this border with France, Luxembourg, Belgium, and the Netherlands.

In 1651, an Estonian man named Hans was tried for being a werewolf. Hans confessed and said he had been bitten by a man dressed in black. He described himself as feeling like a wild beast when he transformed. Hans was sentenced to death.

Many people believed the man in Hans's story was the devil.

Between 1764 and 1767, more than 100 people were attacked and killed in Gévaudan, France. Many people blamed a werewolf. Soldiers hunted and killed more than 100 wolves in the area. Finally, a local hunter shot and killed a wolflike creature with a huge head. The killings stopped. It is still a mystery what caused the deaths and what the wolflike creature was.

Some historians believe the Gévaudan beast was a young male lion or a hyena.

CHAPTER 6
LYCANTHROPY

XTREME FACT

Some people thought you could become a werewolf if you drank water from a wolf's paw print or ate a wolf's brain.

Some legends say that becoming a werewolf is due to a curse. Others claim that people become werewolves after being scratched or bitten by one. But there is another reason people may think they are werewolves. It is a mental illness called clinical lycanthropy. This is when a person believes they have turned into a wolf or another animal.

In 2016, Austin Harrouff (*center*) killed two people while believing he was half animal. He was later diagnosed with clinical lycanthropy.

The first case of clinical lycanthropy was diagnosed in 1852. A French man was convinced that he had turned into a wolf. He believed he had long, scruffy fur. He only wanted to eat rotten, raw meat. Today, doctors believe most clinical lycanthropy cases result from **schizophrenia** or **depression**.

People with lycanthropy often have visual delusions. They may see themselves transform into wolves when they look in a mirror.

CHAPTER 7

OTHER SCIENTIFIC EXPLANATIONS

Petrus Gonsalvus (*left*) had one of the first recorded cases of hypertrichosis.

Physical illnesses may also have fueled werewolf myths. The disease hypertrichosis causes people to grow thick hair over their whole body. Cushing's syndrome is another disease that causes people to grow a lot of hair. Cushing's syndrome also makes a person's face and hands grow larger, and they may become agitated.

In 1725, a boy was found wandering on all fours through a German forest. Many thought he was a werewolf or raised by wolves. They called him Peter the Wild Boy. Scientists now believe that Peter had Pitt-Hopkins syndrome. It is a **genetic** condition that causes extra hair growth and **distinctive** facial features.

XTREME FACT

Peter briefly lived at Kensington Palace in England after he was found. He then lived on a farm until his death in 1785.

Peter was brought to King George I of Great Britain by locals. King George then brought Peter to London, England.

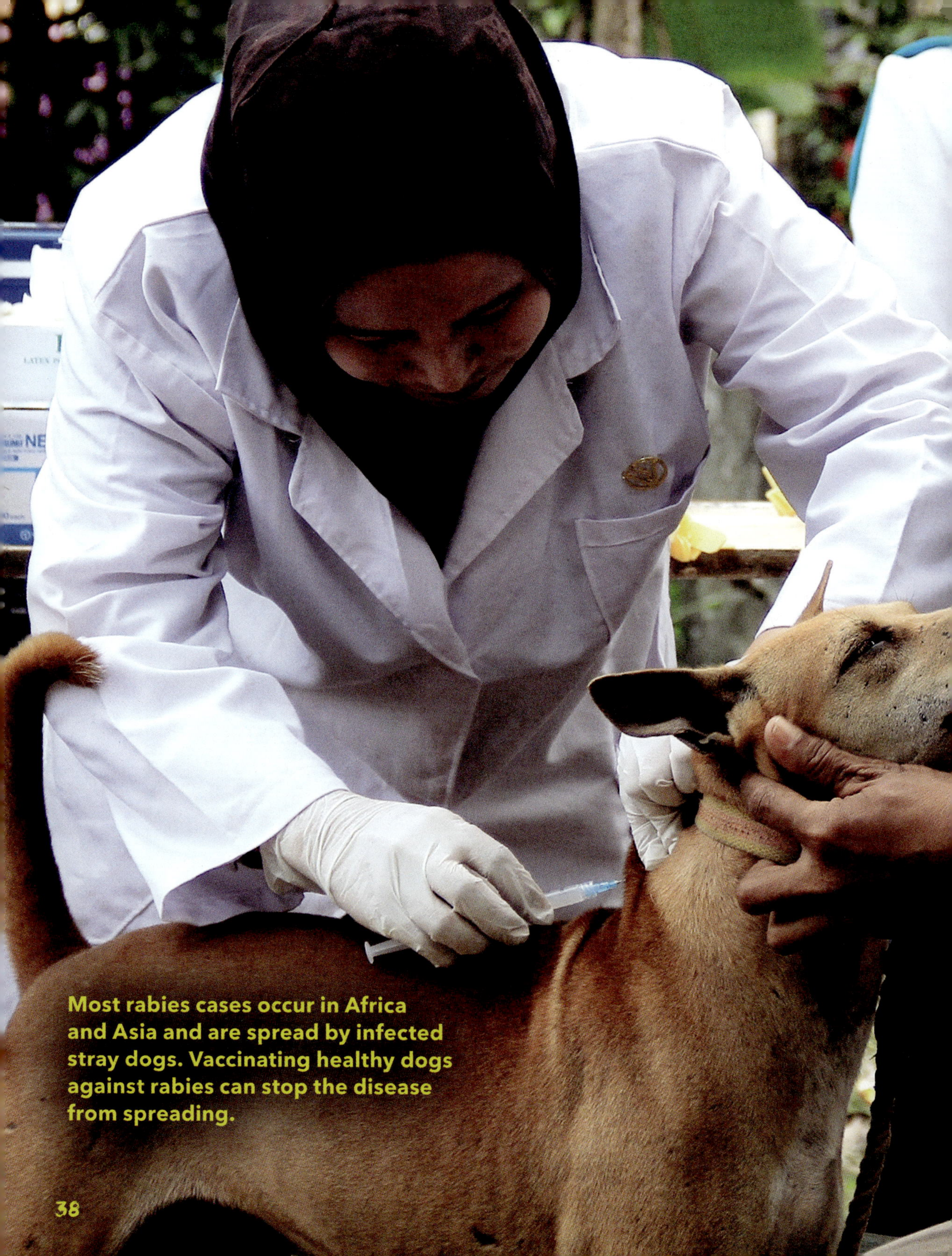

Most rabies cases occur in Africa and Asia and are spread by infected stray dogs. Vaccinating healthy dogs against rabies can stop the disease from spreading.

Many werewolves may have been people or animals with rabies. Rabies is a disease transmitted through the rabies virus. People get the virus after being bitten by an **infected** animal, such as a wolf. Many rabies symptoms describe werewolf behavior. These include increased **aggression** and bloody **saliva**.

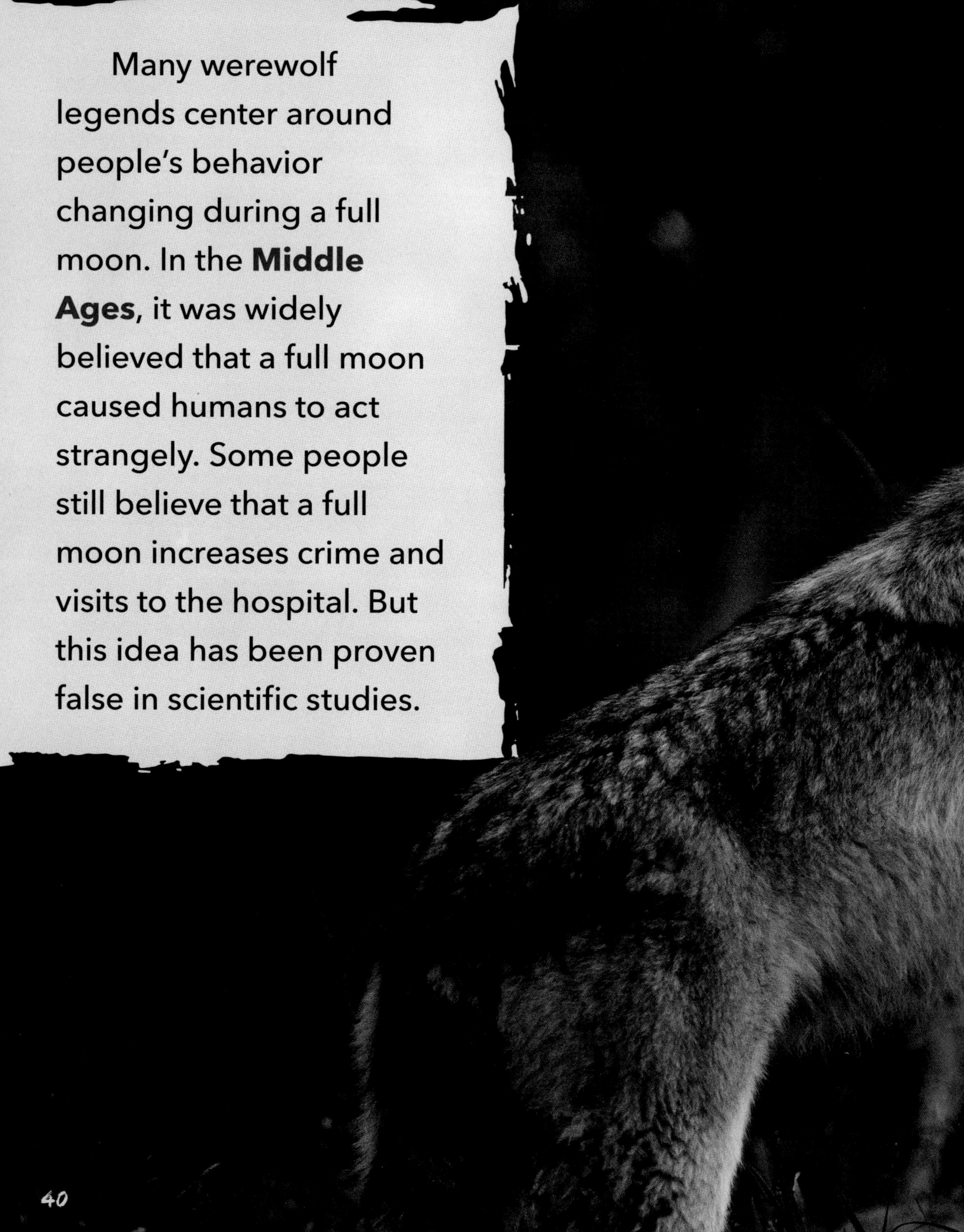

Many werewolf legends center around people's behavior changing during a full moon. In the **Middle Ages**, it was widely believed that a full moon caused humans to act strangely. Some people still believe that a full moon increases crime and visits to the hospital. But this idea has been proven false in scientific studies.

People used to believe that wolves only howled during a full moon. But wolves can howl at any time of day. They do this to communicate with other wolves.

CHAPTER 8

SCIENCE VS. STORIES

Werewolf stories have **evolved** over hundreds of years. The stories often tried to explain death, disease, and the fear of wolves. Science can now explain the facts behind these myths. But werewolf stories are still here today. Do you believe in werewolves?

TAKE THE QUIZ BELOW AND
PUT WHAT YOU'VE LEARNED TO THE TEST!

1) What is a werewolf?

2) Why do you think people believed in werewolves?

3) What are skinwalkers?

4) What diseases and conditions are associated with werewolves?

5) After reading this book, do you believe in werewolves?

WEREWOLF HORROR LAB

A wolf's (and possibly a werewolf's) strongest sense is smell. A wolf can smell its prey from almost 2 miles (3.2 km) away in good weather.

WHAT YOU NEED

- 4 small containers with lids
- 4 smelly items, such as garlic, vinegar, mint, and vanilla
- partner
- blindfold
- tape measure
- notebook
- pen or pencil

WHAT YOU DO

1. Fill each container with a smelly item and close the lid.
2. Blindfold your partner. Stand 25 feet (7.6 m) apart.

3 Open one of the containers. Ask if your partner can smell anything. Have them take one step forward if they can't. Repeat this process until your partner can guess the smell correctly.

4 Use a tape measure to determine how many feet away your partner was when they guessed the smell correctly. Record the distance in your notebook.

5 Repeat steps 2 through 4 with the remaining containers. From what distance could your partner identify the smells? Were some smells easier to detect than others?

TAKE IT FURTHER!

Repeat the project with new smelly items. But this time, you guess the smells! Were you able to identify the items from farther away than your partner? What might this say about your sense of smell?

GLOSSARY

aggression–forceful or hostile actions.

depression–a state of feeling sad or dejected.

distinctive–having a special feature that sets one apart from the others.

evolve–to develop gradually.

genetic–of or relating to a branch of biology that deals with inherited features.

infected–to have a disease caused by bacteria or other germs.

Middle Ages–a period in European history that lasted from about 500 CE to about 1500 CE.

mythology–a collection of myths from a certain group of people.

pasture–land used for grazing.

saliva–a liquid produced in the mouth. It keeps the mouth moist and helps in chewing, swallowing, and breaking down food.

schizophrenia—a mental illness in which a person does not know what sights, sounds, and experiences are real or what they are imagining.

shape-shifter—a mythical figure that is able to change into different forms.

torture—to cause strong physical or mental pain for a purpose, such as gaining information.

witchcraft—the use of sorcery or magic.

ONLINE RESOURCES

To learn more about werewolves, please visit **abdobooklinks.com** or scan this QR code. These links are routinely monitored and updated to provide the most current information available.

INDEX